I Can Tell Time

At the Zoo
Telling Time by the Quarter Hour

by Alice Proctor

WEEKLY READER®
PUBLISHING

Math and Curriculum
Debra Voege, M.A.,
Science and Math Curriculum Resource Teacher

Please visit our web site at: www.garethstevens.com
For a free color catalog describing our list of high-quality books,
call 1-800-542-2595 (USA) or 1-800-387-3178 (Canada).

Library of Congress Cataloging-in-Publication Data

Proctor, Alice, 1967-
    At the zoo: telling time by the quarter hour / Alice Proctor.
      p. cm. — (I can tell time)
    ISBN-10: 0-8368-8391-8 — ISBN-13: 978-0-8368-8391-6 (lib. bdg.)
    ISBN-10: 0-8368-8396-9 — ISBN-13: 978-0-8368-8396-1 (softcover)
    1. Time—Juvenile literature. 2. Zoos—Juvenile literature. I. Title.
QB209.5.P769   2007
529'.7—dc22   2007017439

This North American edition first published in 2008 by
Weekly Reader® Books
An imprint of Gareth Stevens Publishing
1 Reader's Digest Road
Pleasantville, NY 10570-7000 USA

This U.S. edition copyright © 2008 by Gareth Stevens, Inc. Original
edition copyright © 2007 by ticktock Entertainment Ltd. First published
in Great Britain in 2007 by ticktock Media Ltd., Unit 2, Orchard Business
Centre, North Farm Road, Tunbridge Wells, Kent, TN2 3XF, United Kingdom.

Gareth Stevens series editor: Dorothy L. Gibbs
Gareth Stevens graphic design and cover design: Dave Kowalski
Gareth Stevens art direction: Tammy West

Picture credits: (t=top, b=bottom, c=center, l=left, r=right)
Alamy: 1, 9t, 13 both, 14–15 background, 17b, 23tl, 23tr. Banana
Stock: 19b. Corbis: 23br. Istock: 20 both. Jupiter Images/FoodPix: 11t.
Shutterstock: cover, 11b, 12, 15t, 17t, 21, 22 all, 23bl, 24br. Superstock:
4t, 10, 15b, 16, 18, 19t. Ticktock Media Archive: 4b, 5 all, 6, 7 both, 8,
9b, 24bl.

Every effort has been made to trace the copyright holders for
the pictures used in this book. We apologize in advance for any unintentional
omissions and would be pleased to insert the appropriate acknowledgements
in any subsequent edition.

Printed in the United States of America

1 2 3 4 5 6 7 8 9 11 10 09 08 07

Contents

Glossary words are printed in **boldface** type in the text.

Telling Time

Hooray, it is Saturday! We are going to the zoo. I have been waiting to go all week.

The zoo has so many things to see and do. Let's make sure we know how to tell time. We don't want to miss anything!

What time is it?

The little hand on a clock shows what **hour** it is. The big hand shows how many **minutes** it is before or after the hour. The big hand on 12 always means "**o'clock**."

The little hand on this clock is pointing at the 3, so the time is 3 o'clock.

What time is it now?

On this watch, the little hand has passed the 3, and the big hand is pointing at the 6. The big hand has moved halfway around the clock, so the time is **half past** 3.

Can you tell the time on these clocks?

Instead of half past 3, we sometimes say three-thirty.

Quarter Past

Look! The big hand is pointing at the 3. Do you know what time is it now?

Quarter Past 12

Look closely at this clock. The little hand is pointing just past the 12. The big hand is pointing at the 3.

The big hand has moved one-quarter of the way around the clock,  so the time is **quarter past** 12.

Remember, when the big hand is on the 3, the time is quarter past.

Quarter Past 1

Here, the little hand is pointing just past the 1. The big hand is pointing at the 3. The time on this clock is quarter past 1.

Digital Clocks

A digital clock does not have hands. Instead, It shows two numbers. The first number is the hour. The second is the number of minutes past the hour.

On this watch, the hour is 8 o'clock. The number of minutes past 8 o'clock is 15. Because 15 minutes is a **quarter of an hour**, the time is quarter past 8.

Instead of quarter past 8, we sometimes say eight-fifteen.

Quarter To

Now the big hand is pointing at the 9. The little hand has moved, too!

Quarter To 5

On this watch, the little hand is almost pointing at the 5, and the big hand is pointing at the 9.

The big hand has to move around only one more quarter of the clock face to get to the number 12. When the big hand points to 12, the time will be 5 o'clock. But, right now, the time is **quarter to** 5.

Remember, when the big hand is on the 9, the time is quarter to.

Quarter To 9

The big hand on this clock is pointing at the 9. The little hand is almost at the 9, too. On this clock, the time is quarter to 9.

Digital Clocks

The time on this digital clock is 45 minutes past 8 o'clock.

Each hour has 60 minutes. After 45 minutes pass, the time left until the next hour is 15 minutes, or a quarter of an hour. The next hour will be 9 o'clock, so the time on this digital clock is quarter to 9.

Instead of quarter to 9, we sometimes say eight forty-five.

My Day at the Zoo

The alarm clock is ringing.
I get up right away! I am
so excited about going
to the zoo today.

Time for Breakfast

Half past 7

Mom made pancakes for
breakfast. After I eat, it
will be time to brush my
teeth and get dressed.

Time to Get Ready

Quarter past 8

Dad is making sandwiches for our lunch at the zoo. He says we have to leave in 45 minutes.

Time to Go

It is 9'clock. We are ready to go. We walk quickly to meet the bus. It leaves in 15 minutes!

Morning at the Zoo

We're here! We are at the zoo. The bus ride took **half an hour**. Let's go see the monkeys first!

Monkey Time

10 o'clock
It takes us 15 minutes to find the monkeys. Now the time is 10 o'clock.

Look at the baby monkey on its mother's back!

Is this monkey still eating breakfast?

Just in Time

Quarter to 11

When we get to the elephants, it is quarter to 11. We are lucky to see the last elephant getting its bath. Bath time started at 10:15.

High Time for Lunch

Half past 11

At 11:30, we see a giraffe eating twigs and leaves. It must be almost lunchtime!

What time do you eat lunch?

Feeding Time at the Zoo

Watching the giraffe eat makes us hungry. At **noon**, we find a place to sit down and eat our lunch.

Fish for Lunch

Half past 12

We watch the penguins while we eat. They are eating, too. We are eating sandwiches. The penguins are eating fish.

Late Lunch
Quarter past 1

At one-fifteen, the panda is still eating lunch. Pandas eat a lot. Bamboo is their favorite food. We watch the panda eat bamboo for half an hour!

Tiger Time
Quarter to 2

Next, we look for the tiger. I see it! The tiger is hiding in the long grass. It's stripes make it hard to see.

After 12 o'clock noon, times are called "p.m."

15

Afternoon at the Zoo

My day at the zoo is going by quickly. We're getting a little tired, but there are still so many animals to see!

Time to Rest

Half past 2

Dad says we can rest while we watch the sharks. They are swimming in a big tank of water called an aquarium. Look how huge they are!

Quiet Time

3 o'clock

We visit the lions next. Look! The mother lion and her cubs are resting. They must be tired, too.

Rhino Watching

Quarter to 4

Quick! We have only 15 minutes left to see the rhinoceros. The bus leaves at 4 o'clock!

Remember that 15 minutes is a quarter of an hour.

On the ride home, we talk about zoo animals. I liked the lion. Mom liked the giraffe. Dad liked the sharks.

Back Home

Quarter to 5

When we get home, Mom starts making dinner. It will be dinnertime in 45 minutes.

Time for Dinner

Half past 5

While we eat dinner, Mom tells me more about zoos. She says that zoos take care of many animals that cannot survive on their own in the wild.

Bedtime

Quarter past 7

I take my cuddly new lion to bed with me. It is a quarter of an hour before my bedtime, but I am very, very tired. I had a fun day at the zoo.

What time do you go to bed?

Time Facts

There are lots of things to know about hours and minutes. Here are some of them.

> ## Hours
> Each day has 24 hours.

Times between 12 o'clock **midnight** and 12 o'clock noon end in a.m., so at 3:30 a.m., you are asleep!

Times between noon and midnight end in p.m., so 3:30 p.m. is in the middle of the afternoon.

Minutes
Each hour has 60 minutes.

After 15 minutes, it is quarter past the hour.

After 45 minutes, it is quarter to the next hour.

After 30 minutes, it is half past the hour.

Each minute has 60 seconds.

Times to Remember

Try these fun puzzles to show what you know about time.

Mealtime Matchup
Match each meal with the time of day you would eat it.

lunch

breakfast

dinner

7:30 a.m.

1:00 p.m.

5:30 p.m.

Time It Game!

Try to guess how much time it takes you to do each of the activities below. Then ask an adult to time you, using a clock or a watch.

Brush your teeth.

Get dressed.

Eat breakfast.

Clean your bedroom.

Do you have your own clock or watch?

Glossary

a.m. – the abbreviation used with times of the day between midnight and noon (9:00 a.m. is 9 o'clock in the morning)

half an hour – 30 minutes, or half of the 60 minutes in 1 hour

half past – any time when the big hand on a clock is pointing exactly at the 6, showing that half an hour has passed

hour – a measure of time that equals 60 minutes. Each day has 24 hours.

midnight – the 12 o'clock hour in the middle of the night

minutes – measures of time that equal 60 seconds. Each hour has 60 minutes.

noon – the 12 o'clock hour in the middle of the day

o'clock – any hour of the day when the big hand on a clock is pointing exactly at the 12. The little hand shows what hour it is.

p.m. – the abbreviation used with times of the day between noon and midnight (9:00 p.m. is 9 o'clock at night)

quarter of an hour – 15 minutes, or one-quarter of the 60 minutes in 1 hour

quarter past – any time when the big hand on a clock is pointing exactly at the 3, showing that a quarter of an hour has passed

quarter to – any time when the big hand on a clock is pointing exactly at the 9, showing that it is only a quarter of an hour until the next hour begins

week – a measure of time that equals 7 days

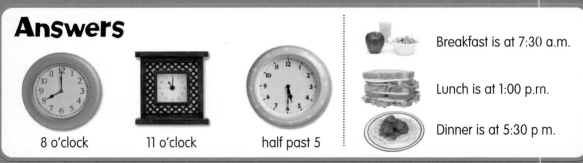

Answers

8 o'clock   11 o'clock   half past 5

Breakfast is at 7:30 a.m.

Lunch is at 1:00 p.m.

Dinner is at 5:30 p.m.